Deonna Baney

Children's Book Author

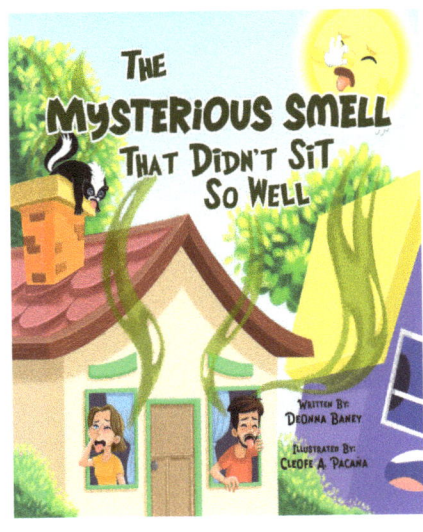

The Mysterious Taste, But I'm Not Supposed To Waste

Written By: Deonna Baney

Illustrated By: Cleofe A. Pacana

DEDICATION

In loving memory of my father, Leon Benjamin Hollis, Sr. and my father-in-law, Stan Baney and my mother-in-law, Betty Baney

It was just another day,
or so I thought.
That is until I didn't eat the food
that was brought.

As you get older oftentimes
you can be bolder.
But sometimes your parents will
tap you on the shoulder.

What is with the tap,
you ask?
It is often to ask you
to finish a task.

This particular task is to finish your food with no questions asked.

When Mommy puts down the plate,
I wonder if it will taste great.

Here I go, I take a bite.
Hoping that it will be a delight.

But what is this taste in my face?
No, no, no, it isn't your face
in which you use to taste.

You use your mouth and
then the food travels south.

My tongue is coated with a lie
that my parents floated.

This is a taste that I wish I could erase!
But I left my erasers at school.
Mommy and Daddy, this just isn't cool.

I wait for my parents
to look away.
When they do, I know
just what to say.

"Mommy and Daddy, this is a taste
I have never had before."
This is something that you can say
when you are four, but now I am nine,
and that is not fine.

Daddy says, "Marilyn, you have to try it."
But when I try it, they expect me to eat more!
I'm about to spit out on the floor.

Maybe I can spit it out, but surely that
will make Daddy shout. What if I pout?
No, no, no then they will ask, "What is this all about?"

Oh, my goodness, did I just swallow a fly?
Surely it wasn't a fly,
Mommy can cook, she really does try.

But if I keep eating this,
I am sure I will just die.

Hmmm.... That's it!!
If I can just get the dog to come sit.

She can sit and wait until
I give her everything off my plate!

The dog will eat and eat so that
I don't have to try this mystery meat.

Why would anyone eat something that smells like crusty, dusty, feet?

I still don't know what I ate
from this icky, icky plate.

It is a mysterious taste,
There is no doubt.
But I am not supposed to waste.
So, what is that all about?

How is it fair? Wait, did I just see a hair?
It can't be a hair, they wouldn't dare!

They know I am
ticky and picky.
So, why do they insist
on making my food
extra icky and sticky?

Why a trash can you ask?
Because even the food in there
looks like something that I can bear,
not this thing that makes me just stare.

How is this fair?
Why do I have to sit
here and stare
at this mystery meat
that has possible hair?

Oh wait, here comes the dog.
I am going to give her this food
that looks like a log.

Oh no! Say it isn't so!
The dog even said "NO!"
Well, she didn't actually say no,
but she did stick her nose up
and had to go.

I must find out what this is all about.
I have a mysterious taste that
I am not supposed to waste.,
but my dog even ran away in haste.
Surely, I will have to solve this case.
A hole in the backyard is the only place
that this terrible mystery meat will not be in my face!

But I don't have time to get the shovel.
Even if I did, I would surely be in trouble.

It is absurd that I must stay
when I can't force my mouth
to eat food this way.

Why can't I get them to understand
that the textures of this food ruin that plan?

The taste is different when I bite.
I swear that I don't want
to sit here all night.

Broccoli looks like a tree.

Ginger root looks like an old man's knee.

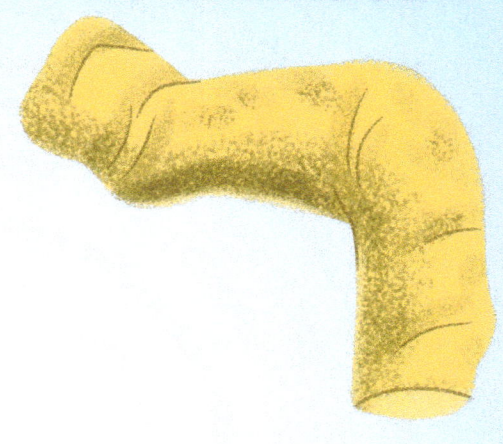

Bananas fool you with bright yellow peels.

But watermelon, well it's just how it feels.

So, what did you put on my plate?
There's white stuff that is sticky like glue.
I think I once had some on an old shoe.

There are green things
that look like
little basketballs.
They smell really bad, and
I think I saw
them once at my Pa's.

The lima beans taste like
old gym socks.
I don't know how I know that,
but I would rather eat rocks!

But worst of all is the
mystery meat,
and the fact that my baby sister
gets to eat sweets!

The dog will not eat it,
and it looks really bad.
I'm not sure what's in it,
but it's making me really sad.

HA!
HA!
HA!

Worst of all, my sister is
laughing and starting
to make me mad.

It is brown, red, green, and white.
And when I think of eating it,
it fills me with fright.
So why, Mommy and Daddy,
must I try a bite?
This really is the most horrible night

I think I have solved the mystery once and for all.
The thing on my plate is meat loaf, and it is too tall.

It is filled with all kinds of things,
but nothing that makes my taste buds sing.

I beg and I plead to not have to suffer.
But I don't want to hurt
the feelings of my mother.

Here it goes. I take a bite.
I pinch my nose and hold on tight.
This has got to be the very worst night!

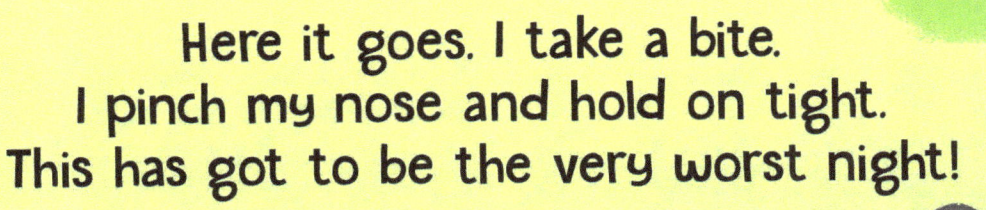

But it turns out
my parents were right.
It actually tastes a little all right
despite the sight.

But I fear that I might not be able
to take another bite,
because it looks and feels like something
that just isn't right.

I decided instead to try
to be good and eat,
because I want to go play
after this feat.

Daddy says, "The longer you take, the more time you waste, so eat up kiddo so we can play chase!"

I gobble it up and
send it downtown.
Then me and sissy
chase daddy all around.

Well, I guess the mysterious
taste wasn't so bad.
My plate is clean, and
I didn't make mommy sad.

The mysterious taste was actually kind of good.
I'm going to start trying new things just like I
should!

But, oh no! I ran too fast!
My food comes up from
out of my tummy in a flash!

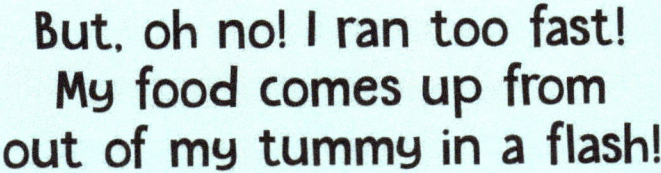

Please don't make me eat any more and
I promise to clean it up off the floor!
After all that fussing, what was it even for?

The End!

Acknowledgements

My husband, Matthew, and my children,
Marilyn, and Scarlett
for always encouraging me to
do better and do more.
Without my family, my inspiration for these stories
would not be as entertaining.

About The Author

Deonna Baney is a wife, mother, and registered nurse who lives in Arkansas. Her dream is to not only take care of others with her current career, but to also touch as many lives as she can through her stories. Making others laugh in their darkest times is what has inspired her to start writing children's stories with the whole family in mind.